Messner Books by Sheila L. Burns
Allergies and You
Cancer: Understanding and Fighting It

Cancer

UNDERSTANDING and FIGHTING IT

SHEILA L. BURNS

JULIAN MESSNER NEW YORK

Manufactured in the United States of America

Design by Stephen Alterwein

Photo Credits

American Cancer Society, pp. 12, 33, 41 top, 42, 45,
47, 48, 51
NCI-"Frontiers of Research", pp. 37, 54
National Institutes of Health, 15, 17, 20, 21, 23, 25,
28, 29, 34, 41 bottom
Cover Photo courtesy American Cancer Society
DRAWINGS BY FRANK LEDOUX

Library of Congress Cataloging in Publication Data

Burns, Sheila L.
   Cancer, understanding and fighting it.

      Includes index.
      Summary: Against a background of a child and
her grandmother who has cancer, the latest knowledge
about cancer is explained.
         1. Cancer—Juvenile literature. [1. Cancer]
I. Title.
RC263.B825   1982   616.99'4   82-8151
ISBN 0-671-44250-3   AACR2

Contents

Most people keep cancer a mystery to youngsters.

1 A Mystery

Mary Ann's mother and aunt began whispering. Mary Ann tried to hear. They were talking about Grandmother.

"Did the doctor's office call today?" her mother asked.

"Yes," Aunt Sally replied, lowering her voice even more. Mary Ann went on clearing the table, but very quietly so that she would not draw attention to herself.

"What was the lab report?" Mother asked.

This time Sally did not reply. Mother turned from the sink to look at her. "Well?" she asked. Sally was wiping the tines of a fork over and over.

Finally, Sally said, "It's cancer."

Mother's face changed. They both glanced toward Mary Ann, but she was working in the other room as if she had not heard. Then it was quiet in the kitchen.

Mary Ann suddenly couldn't stand the silence. "What's the matter with Grandmother?" she asked.

"She hasn't been feeling well lately," said her mother. "We thought maybe the doctor could help her feel better."

Mary Ann knew there was something they were not telling her. But what?

That night everyone wanted to talk with Grandmother. Mary Ann did, too. She slipped her hand under Grandmother's arm and put her head against her shoulder. She never found a chance to ask any questions.

The next afternoon Mary Ann came home from school when everyone else was at work. She had Grandmother to herself. Then she remembered her question.

"Grandmother," she asked, "what is cancer? Do you have cancer?"

"Yes, I do," Grandmother replied.

"How come everybody whispers about it?" asked Mary Ann.

Grandmother said, "Because they don't like to talk about it. They are afraid of it, you see."

"Mother and Aunt Sally wouldn't tell me last night," Mary Ann explained.

"Your mother probably didn't know exactly what to say," Grandmother told her. "I don't understand it very well myself. Nobody really understands it well. That's why people are afraid."

"But cancer is just being sick, isn't it?"

"Well, yes. It's an illness." Grandmother seemed unsure. "It's a very serious illness sometimes. Perhaps the doctor could explain it best. Shall I take you with me the next time I go?"

"Oh, yes," Mary Ann agreed instantly. That way she could ask all the questions she wanted.

"But he did tell me that cancer is not catching," Grandmother went on. "We know *that* much. You won't get it from me. Neither will anyone else in the family. I can still cook for you because there are no cancer germs. It's not that kind of illness."

Suddenly, Grandmother put her arms around Mary Ann and hugged her tight. "I'm not going to give you my illness," she said. "You're my girl."

Mary Ann's parents were surprised to hear Grandmother's plan to take Mary Ann to the doctor with her. "Is it really necessary?" Mother asked.

"Mary Ann is with me every day now that you are working," Grandmother reminded her. "In fact, I probably spend more time with Mary Ann than with anyone else. Naturally she has questions. And I don't have the answers."

So it was settled. On Grandmother's next doctor's appointment, Mary Ann would go, too.

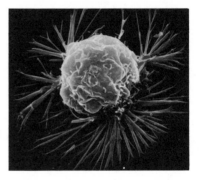

Human cancer cell seen through an electron microscope.

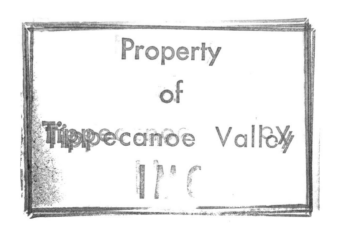

2 1,000,000,000,000 Cells—All In Perfect Order

The doctor leaned back and made a tent with his fingers. "What is cancer?" he repeated Grandmother's question. "Well, first of all, it's a disease of the cells. Do you know what cells are?" he asked Mary Ann.

"Um," replied Mary Ann uncertainly, "Not really."

The doctor looked thoughtful. Mary Ann could see that this was a big subject. "We human beings and every other living thing, from trees right through the whole plant and animal kingdom, are all made of cells. Just as a building may be made of thousands of bricks, the human body is made up of cells—about 60 trillion of them. A cell is the smallest possible living thing."

Mary Ann looked puzzled. The doctor lifted a finger. "Wait a minute. We'll show you. Harold!" he called. A young man in a white coat appeared at the door. "I want you to show this young lady what cells look like while I talk to her grandmother."

Mary Ann followed Harold into another room where a microscope was set on a table. He took a piece of glass from a rack and put it under the microscope.

"On here is a sample of cells from a human being," Harold told her. "We put them between two pieces of glass so we can look at them. Here, let me set up the microscope for you."

As Mary Ann looked through the lens, Harold told her what she was seeing. "Cells look different according

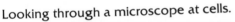

Looking through a microscope at cells.

to what part of the body they come from," he said. He pulled out other pieces of glass with cells on them and put them one by one under the microscope. He pointed out what to look at with his pencil.

Mary Ann asked, "How do you know these things are cells? I mean, we might be looking at a piece of your pencil, or a fleck of dirt. If you can't see it, how do you know?"

"No piece of lead or dirt acts like a living cell," Harold told her. "Lead can't move or reproduce—make another like itself. If I see one cell suddenly split into two, I *know* it must be alive. It can't be a mineral like lead. *Only* living things reproduce."

"Are you sure?" asked Mary Ann.

"Absolutely," Harold declared. "Each one of us came from a cell no bigger than the one you're looking at, though a different kind. That cell bulged and spread out. Then the middle got thinner, and then—POP! It split in two and there were two cells, exactly alike. Then each of the two cells split, and there were four cells.

"As the cells kept on splitting, some cells turned into skin cells, some cells became bone, some hair, some heart. Eventually a whole body existed with each cell in its proper place. We all came to life like that."

"The cells seem to be very smart to do all that by themselves," Mary Ann said. "I mean—" Suddenly she felt confused. A body could not build itself, could it?

Harold seemed to understand. "We don't know exactly how it happens. But we do know that cell reproduction goes on whenever we need it, even though we don't know it's happening. Right now, you and I are reproducing cells to replace worn-out cells. If human beings were clever enough," he went on, "we could look at a cell and tell from whom it came. A cell is *that* special."

Just then Grandmother and the doctor came into the laboratory. Then Mary Ann remembered why she was there. "I've been finding out all about cells, but I didn't learn a thing about cancer!" she exclaimed.

The doctor and Harold smiled. "Oh, yes, you did," the doctor told her. "Cancer is a problem of how cells reproduce. Instead of splitting just when new cells are needed, a cancer cell keeps on splitting without stopping. It spread out in all directions. Cancer cells form a mass that crowds normal cells and chokes them to death. If too many normal cells die, the person dies, too.

"A cancer cell is an outlaw cell," he went on. "It does not work for the health of the body it belongs to, but just for itself. We have to get rid of it, or it will take over."

"That's why cancer is not contagious," Grandmother reminded Mary Ann. "It is not a germ that comes from outside. It is one of our own cells gone wrong."

"Why does a cell do that?" Mary Ann wondered.

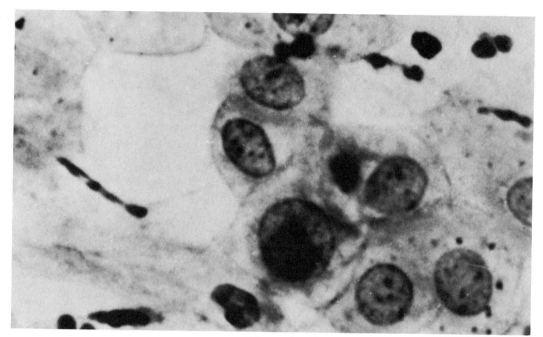

Normal cell.

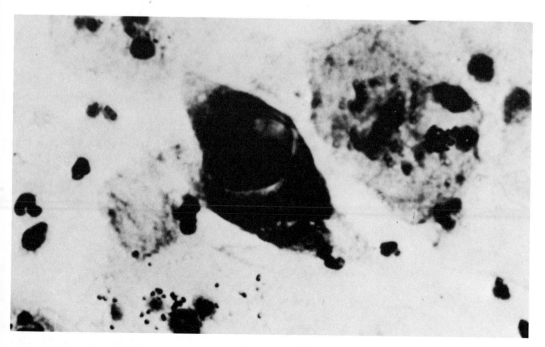

Cancer cell.

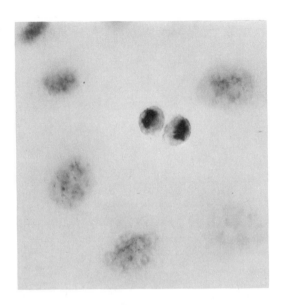

The same cell seen through a light microscope. The darker center, the nucleus, has divided in two.

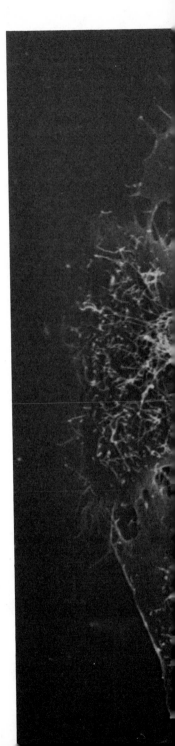

Cancer cell dividing, as seen through an electron microscope.

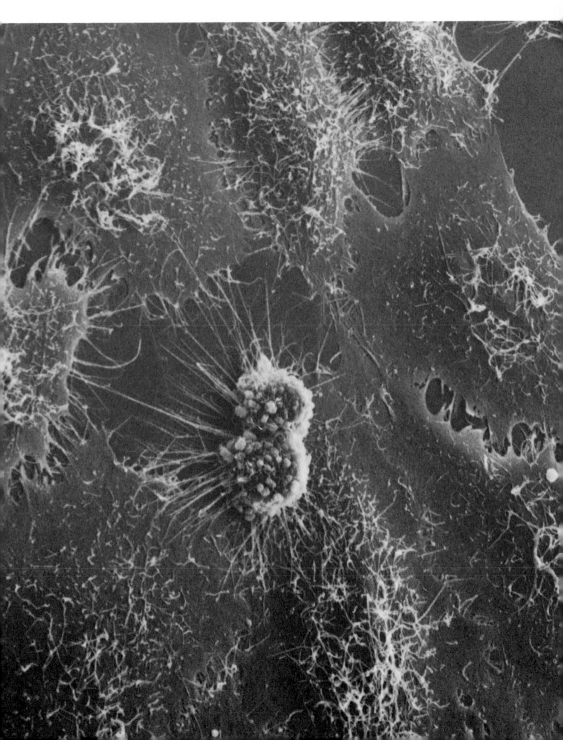

"We don't really know, though we have some good ideas," the doctor told her. "Meanwhile, we can help your grandmother. She will have an operation. A surgeon will take out the mass of cancerous cells. Grandmother will have other treatments, too. Then, if the cancer has not metastasized, it should be stopped."

"What is 'metastasized'?" Mary Ann asked.

"It's a big word that means 'spread'," the doctor replied. "In the beginning, a cancer stays where it starts and just grows bigger. But eventually a few cancer cells break off and move into the bloodstream. This stream of blood carries the cancer cells to other places in the body. Wherever these cells fall, new cancers sprout up. I think and hope that we have caught your grandmother's cancer in the early stage, before it has metastasized."

On the way home, Mary Ann told Grandmother, "I will visit you in the hospital."

"I hope you will be able to," answered Grandmother.

3 Each Cell Has A Life Of Its Own

Grandmother was home and resting after the operation. "The incision, the cut the surgeon made to get at the cancer, needs to heal," Grandmother said to Mary Ann.

"Your skin cells are making new skin," answered Mary Ann, remembering her visit to the doctor's laboratory. "Cells must be wonderfully made to know which ones need to reproduce and when."

Understanding cell reproduction is a puzzle even for scientists. As Mary Ann could see under the microscope, every cell has a *nucleus* or core. In the nucleus are sticklike *chromosomes* scattered around as if they've been dropped accidentally. Chromosomes are rodlike bodies that hold genes. *Genes* determine the characteristics inherited by new living things. Just before a cell reproduces, the chromosomes bunch together at opposite sides of the nucleus. When the cell splits, one set of chromosomes goes with each cell.

The genes in the chromosomes are much too small to

see well, even under an electron microscope. But the cause of cancer lies there, somewhere in the genes.

Genes are made of *deoxyribonucleic acid,* or *DNA* for short. DNA is a group of chemicals clumped together in positions that form a definite pattern. Though we cannot see these patterns, we know what some of them are. Scientists working with tiny beams of light figured them out from reflections. How? Well, suppose you roll a ball across the floor until it is out of sight under a sofa. Then it rolls back at you. You can tell whether it hit something under the sofa. You can tell how it hit—head on, or at the side—by the angle at which the ball comes rolling back. Figuring this *angle of bounce* is the skill of games such as basketball and pool. Scientists figure the angle of bounce of light beams and this tells them the shape of a gene which nobody can see.

These stringy loops are part of a strand of DNA. Genes are made of strands like these. Each strand is a combination of molecules in a particular pattern that tells a cell what to do.

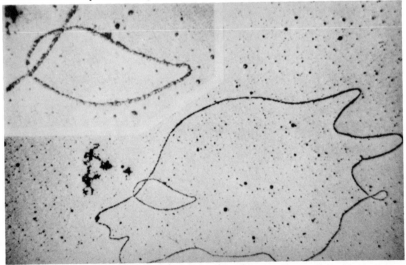

NORMAL CELL

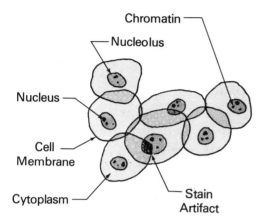

Chromatin

Nucleolus

Nucleus

Cell Membrane

Cytoplasm

Stain Artifact

CANCER CELL

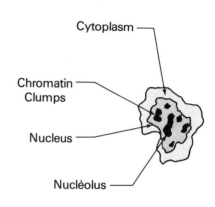

Cytoplasm

Chromatin Clumps

Nucleus

Nucleolus

Normal Cell

Cluster of normal intermediate cells. Note the 1) relatively large amount of cytoplasm 2) clear nuclear stain 3) fine chromatin granules in the nucleus 4) small nucleolus 5) the smooth nuclear boarder 6) stain artifact in one cell where another small white blood cell overlaps.

Cancer Cell

Note 1) large size of the nucleus compared to the total cell size 2) the dark staining of the nucleus 3) the larger size of the chromatin clumps in the nucleus 4) the large nucleolus 5) irregular nuclear boarder.

But if we could zoom in on a gene and take a good look, we expect to see a pattern called a *double helix*. A curl wrapped around your finger is a *helix*. When you withdraw your finger, the curl is in a corkscrew shape. A double helix is like a ladder wrapped into a long curl. It is two corkscrews connected by crossbars.

The ladder and its steps or crossbars are made up of chemicals. The exact arrangement of these chemicals and their sequences, step after step, control everything that happens in a cell. They are like the punched sheet of a

THE DOUBLE HELIX

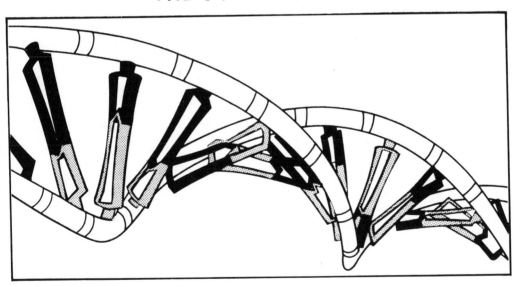

piano roll that makes a player piano strike the notes of a tune. When a cell divides and each new cell has the same chromosomes and therefore the same genes, that cell "plays" the same "tune."

In this way cell reproduction makes sure that every new cell acts exactly as its parent did. It ensures that new cells become new skin, new blood, or whatever they are supposed to be.

This pattern was discovered by the scientists Francis Crick, M. H. F. Wilkins, and J. D. Watson. The discovery won them the Nobel Prize for Medicine in 1962. Since then the study of genes has been perhaps the most exciting field in biology.

Because the genes in a single human cell probably number well over a million, this study may appear very difficult. However, each gene is made up of the same chemicals, only in different arrangements. In fact, the genes of all living things seem to be made of the same substance—DNA. This fact makes it possible for scientists to substitute one gene for another in their studies.

The better understanding of cells gives us hope that we may someday understand cancer, for cancer is a mistake in cell reproduction. If one tiny piece in the helix pattern of chemicals is out of place, it changes the gene. The gene changes the cell, perhaps making it cancerous, perhaps not. The descendants of a changed cell carry the same change in their genes, generation after generation.

This change may never matter since a cell does not do everything it can do—it does not "play" all the possible "tunes." Some differences may even be helpful. But most probably are not.

What can change one tiny molecule—linked as it is into a long chain and folded up small and deep inside a cell? What can reach into such a hidden place? Scientists think that rays from the sun could be one cause. Another cause is the kind of ray that comes from X-rays. Still another cause could be too much exposure to a chemical, as happens to workers in some factories. Viruses, which are partly made of DNA—the same matter that is in a cell's nucleus—may be a cause. Scientists wonder if a virus can somehow knit itself into a cell's core and change its gene or genetic structure.

Scientists are sure that some viruses, radiation, and several hundred chemicals cause cancer in animals. In human beings, too, radiation and chemicals or mixtures of chemicals cause cancer. It seems likely that viruses will prove to have a role, also.

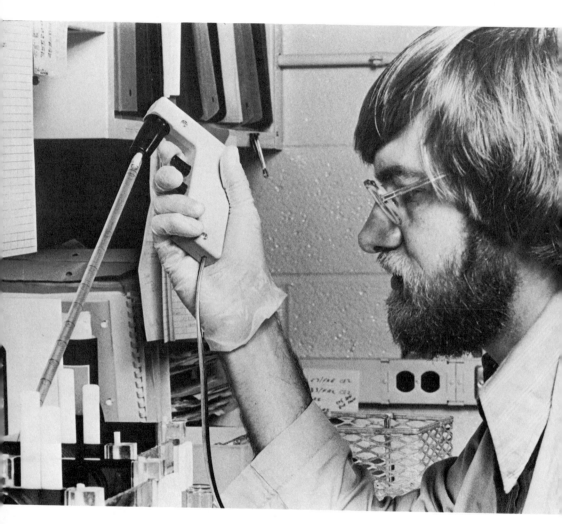

This technician is studying cancer viruses.

It is hard to pinpoint the exact cause of a specific cancer among so many suspected ones. Cancers are different according to the tissue they come from. Probably there is not just one cause but a number of different causes that must work together or in sequence.

However, we do not have to know all the causes to stop cancer. All we really have to do is to stop the cancer cell's lawless reproduction.

Scientists have discovered that too much sun can cause skin cancer in later life. Thus youngsters should use a light cover-up.

4 The Body Sends A Posse After Outlaws

Some scientists believe that the body has built-in ways to get rid of cancer cells. The body may do this through the *immune system*. The immune system is a complicated way that the body protects every one of its cells. When a germ attacks a cell, other cells come to defend it.

Only certain cells are born to be protectors. Defense is their main job—their career, in a way, just as some people in a society are police officers or firemen or garbage collectors. They make a living taking care of the rest of us. The body has certain cells like that, especially in the blood. These cells take care of the rest of the body.

Certain special cells and chemicals in the body locate sick or dead or malformed cells—garbage or refuse that the body has to get rid of. These special cells break up the refuse and carry it away. Other special cells are killers that find enemy germs and viruses and eat them up. Some chemicals in our bodies also kill enemies by poking holes in them.

The cells and chemicals that protect us work together. They have several lines of defense so that if one kind of cell fails, another takes over. These cells and chemicals

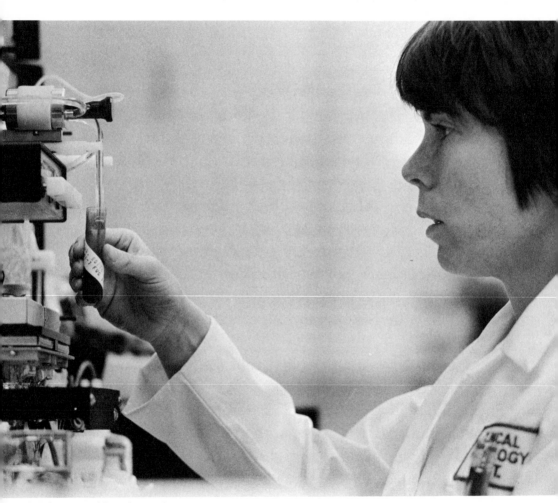

Analyzing a blood specimen.

are linked in a kind of message system. This whole plan is called the *immune system*.

The immune system has several lines of defense with armies of special cells: the "soldiers." The millions of soldiers or protector cells and chemicals of the immune system come from special glands or from the insides of bones. Many enter the blood. They circle through the body, flooding every tissue. That is how the body rids itself of most germs and poisons. It is a kind of rinsing or cleaning.

A lymphocyte, one of the cells of the immune system which help protect against disease.

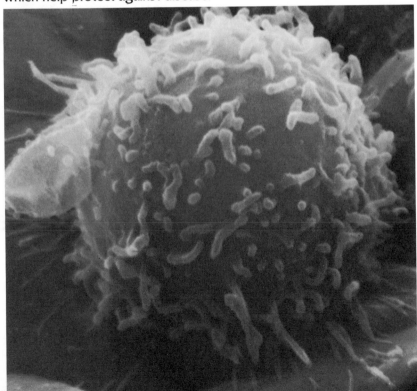

The immune system probably spots cancer cells just as it spots other bad cells. Cancer cells may be swept away routinely along with the everyday trash collection of dead cells and excreted wastes. But perhaps, once in a while, one cancer cell escapes this trash collection.

The immune system catches every virus and germ, and yet it can miss a cancerous cell, which is larger. There must be some reason, but we don't know yet what that reason is. Perhaps a cancer cell has a coating that cloaks the fact that it is not normal. Something on the cell's surface may cover up or smooth over the places where the chemicals of the immune system latch on.

Another hint for *immunologists*—scientists who study the immune system—is the fact that cancer occurs much more often among older people than among the young. Perhaps the immune system starts breaking down as we get older. It may get lazy, not making the cells and chemicals the body needs as fast as it used to. But even in young people, the immune system can go out of order for a while. Maybe cancer gets started then.

Immunology—the study of how the body resists disease —is one of the newer sciences. Doctors do not yet know exactly how to strengthen the immune system. Most of their methods are experimental. That means that research scientists have to try out new ideas very carefully.

They must test them in laboratories for a long time before they can work on human beings.

When doctors give patients new drugs or new treatments, they watch the patients very closely. After treatment they follow these patients for years to see if a new drug has a delayed effect or side effects that no one predicted. If a drug passes all its tests, then it may become available to other doctors besides research doctors. It can take years to go through this process, even when drugs seem to be working well and more patients need their help desperately.

One treatment being studied now is a drug named *interferon*. Interferon is a chemical that seems to stop the

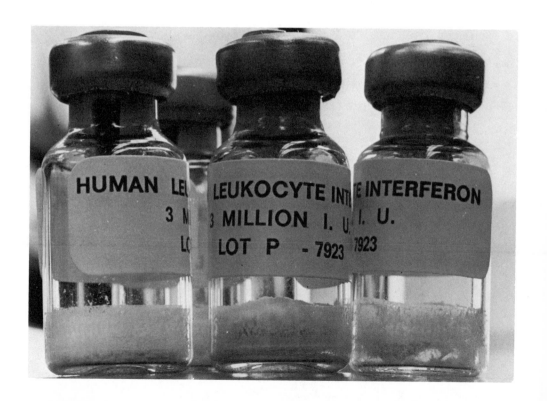

reproduction of some kinds of cancer cells. Every human body makes interferon naturally, but in very small amounts. It takes research pharmacists a long time to produce enough interferon to treat a patient. Therefore the drug is rare and expensive. And right now it is available only to patients who are part of a research study.

But while some researchers study what interferon can do, others are studying ways to make it faster and more cheaply. They have had some success with interferon. So if interferon—or another drug—can be proved to help people, it will soon be available to all who need it.

Some scientists are also trying to better understand why some people recover from cancer naturally. Sometimes a patient's recovery surprises doctors. Sometimes a cancer that appears incurable just vanishes. This does not happen often, but it happens once in a while. Why? Scientists are trying to find out.

Another idea is to find a way to recognize and tag cancer cells. If we could pin a kind of marker on cancer cells, then scientists could produce drugs that act only on those marked cells. That could be a much safer and more efficient treatment than any we have now. But so far it is only a research idea.

This doctor is purifying and concentrating interferon.

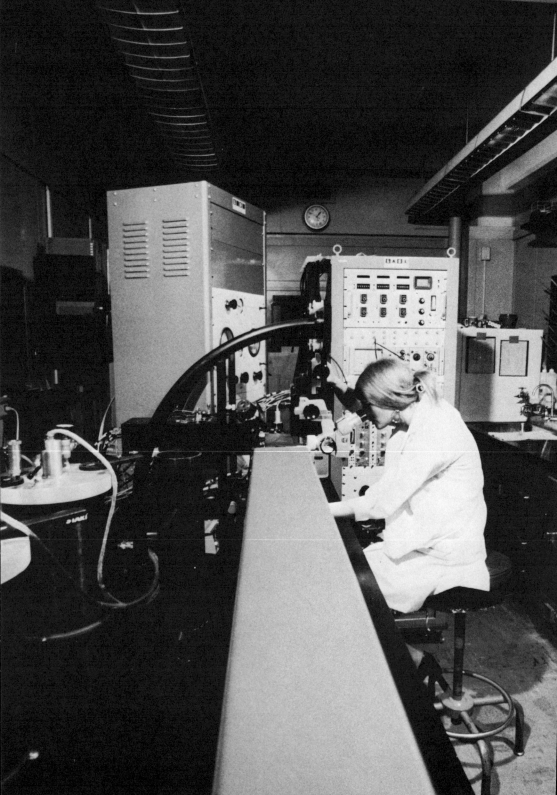

These are just a handful out of hundreds of ideas. Teams of scientists are working on them. But most people who have cancer cannot wait until these ideas are proved right or wrong. They have to use what scientists can offer them right now.

Looking at cancer cells with a special machine which separates and counts them.

5 Getting Back At The Bad Guys

Cancer cells that elude our body's natural defenses may seem powerful and cunning. Nevertheless, when the body's own systems do not win, there are other ways to stop cancer. These are surgery, radiation, and *chemotherapy*—medicines.

Surgery is necessary for many cancers, even when radiation and chemotherapy are also used. Doctors usually remove the cancerous tissue and some of the healthy tissue around it. They have to take out healthy cells in order to make sure that they remove any cancer cells that may have wandered among them. Surgery is most effective when a cancer is small and has not yet metastasized.

Radiation is a flow of particles of energy so small that they can go right through nearly everything. We do not see or feel radiation, but it is happening all the time. The sun is the original source of all the energy on earth—the

Many cancer patients can be cured if surgery is performed early enough.

energy that makes plants grow, that is stored in minerals, and that enables us to grow and develop—to move, talk, and even think. All this energy reaches the earth by radiating, or travelling out from the sun. Sunlight is just one of many kinds of radiation.

Radiation from minerals can be used in treating cancer. In cancer treatments, a machine focuses a beam of radiation from a mineral onto a mass of cancerous cells.

Radiated cells—cancerous and healthy—may die. To prevent healthy tissue from dying, other parts of a patient's body are shielded during radiation. Doctors and nurses shield themselves, too, by wearing a kind of apron made of lead. A barrier of lead is usually built into the wall to protect other people as well. Lead, a dense mineral, keeps mineral radiation from penetrating places where it is not wanted.

Often people who have had an operation to remove a cancer undergo radiation afterward. Cancer cells can escape during an operation. Using radiation, doctors try to make doubly sure to catch every cancerous cell. Sometimes patients have radiation before an operation to make a cancer smaller and easier to remove.

Radiation makes patients feel very tired. They need to rest a great deal. Patients who have radiation also often feel discouraged and frightened. They need help with their feelings as well as their bodies. They need caring and support.

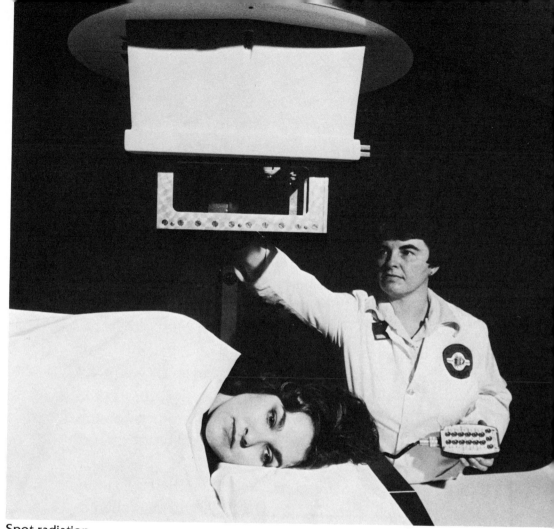

Spot radiation.

Chemotherapy, another major cancer treatment, is the use of drugs to kill cancer cells. Unlike radiation treatments, chemotherapy affects the whole body. It is used against cancers which may have spread from one organ to other parts of the body. Some cancers, such as those that originate in the blood, are so widespread in the body that they cannot be treated by radiation or surgery. Chemotherapy is used for them.

In chemotherapy, drugs are injected into the blood or given by mouth so that they will reach all parts of the body. Doctors calculate the amount given very carefully. They watch a patient closely because these drugs are very dangerous.

Patients taking chemotherapy often feel very sick. They may lose their hair, but only temporarily. The hair grows back as soon as the treatments are over. Just the same, baldness makes a person feel ugly and odd. Patients want to hide from their friends and families, even though they need visitors. But if visitors act naturally and go on talking in the usual way, they can bridge a moment of embarrassment. Soon both the patient and the visitor forget about hair.

Some cancers can be cured by chemotherapy alone. Others can be treated successfully by using chemotherapy with another kind of treatment such as surgery or radiation. Though chemotherapy is not used for every kind of cancer, children's leukemia is one kind that responds well to chemotherapy.

Decisions on how to treat a cancer are a great responsibility and burden for doctors and their patients. None of the treatments is a certain cure. All of them are

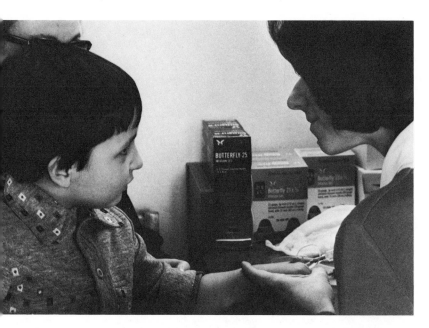

Cancer patients can be of all ages: here, receiving chemotherapy.

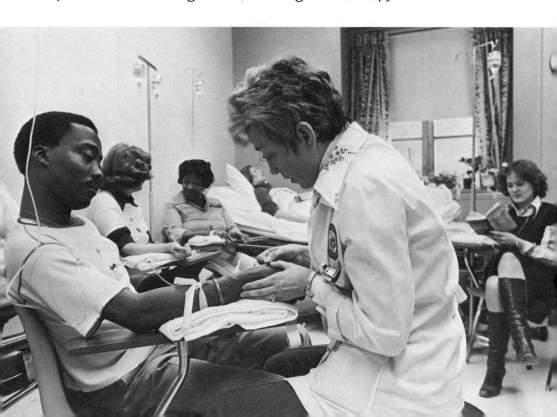

Caring helps.

dangerous, and they can be painful. Patients who are suffering wonder how much they must endure in the hope of getting better. No one—not even the experts—can predict the outcome of a course of treatment. Usually, doctors do not consider a patient cured until five years have passed with no sign of cancer. These uncertainties are hard to bear.

It is natural for a very ill cancer patient to fear dying. A cancer patient who has gotten better probably still thinks of death more often than others do. Sometimes people avoid a cancer patient—even one who has fully recovered —in order to avoid thinking about death. This is natural, too, though maybe it is better to share our human thoughts and fears.

Friends and family members can help a cancer patient simply by being present during a course of treatment and afterward. Friends may feel inadequate because they cannot solve a sick person's problems or console an anxious person. But friends do help. Sharing thoughts and feelings may not be visible help, but it is still very real and comforting.

6 Conquering Cancer

Dr. Lewis Thomas, a well-known cancer specialist and head of the Sloan Kettering Institute for Cancer Research in New York, once predicted that cancer will be conquered by the year 2000. "Conquest" means that most, not all, persons will be cured. In cancer, as in other diseases, a cure depends on an early diagnosis.

Since all human cells are the same in certain basic ways, some people think there are a few basic ways in which all cancers start. Others think that cancers coming from different kinds of cells have different causes. Only research can settle this difference of opinion. During 1981, over 1½ billion dollars from government and other sources was spent on researching a cure for cancer.

Much can be done to prevent cancer even without knowing everything about it. For example, most scientists are convinced that smoking is the most important cause of one kind of cancer—lung cancer. Statistics show

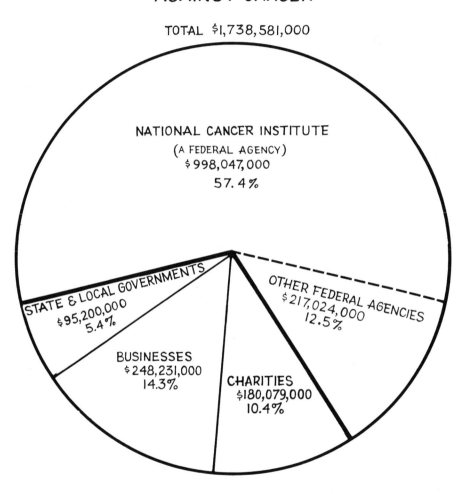

SOURCES OF MONEY FOR THE FIGHT
AGAINST CANCER

TOTAL $1,738,581,000

NATIONAL CANCER INSTITUTE
(A FEDERAL AGENCY)
$998,047,000
57.4%

STATE & LOCAL GOVERNMENTS
$95,200,000
5.4%

OTHER FEDERAL AGENCIES
$217,024,000
12.5%

BUSINESSES
$248,231,000
14.3%

CHARITIES
$180,079,000
10.4%

that people who smoke get cancer more often than others. The longer they smoke, the more likely they are to get cancer.

The evidence is strong enough for nonsmokers and ex-smokers to think all smokers should quit. Yet many go right on smoking. Others begin. Why do they do it? And what can be done about it?

Some people think that a person's bad habits are nobody else's business. They think that people should be allowed to do even harmful things so long as they don't hurt anyone else. But studies show that breathing smoky air hurts even nonsmokers. So smokers may be harmful to others, at least in enclosed places where the smoke cannot drift away.

Smokers insist on smoking just the same, partly because changing any habit is hard. Some people imagine that smoking looks sophisticated and grown-up. To quit, these smokers must be persuaded that quitting is even more sophisticated and more grown-up than continuing.

Persuasion is the only way to achieve other goals, too. People must be encouraged to go to a doctor early enough. Nearly everyone has seen posters that describe early warning signs of cancer. Yet people ignore these symptoms. Even when friends and relatives point out the danger, they pooh-pooh suggestions of alarm. People act

SMOKING IS VERY GLAMOROUS

AMERICAN CANCER SOCIETY

this way because they are afraid. They do not want to hear what a doctor might say.

Early diagnosis could lead to saving the lives of about one out of every six cancer patients. Certainly it is better to make an unnecessary trip to the doctor than to find out too late.

Some scientists think that about eighty percent of all cancers will eventually be traced to overexposure to chemicals. Many of these chemicals are industrial products that did not exist in great quantities or concentrations until this century.

For instance, exhaust gases are in the air from automobiles and factory furnaces. These gases may contain *carcinogens*—cancer-causing chemicals. Some chemicals in water come from run-off of farm fields where they were used as fertilizers or weed-killers. Livestock are being given chemically treated feed. These chemicals are intended to push growth or keep animals healthy. These chemicals remain in the meat when it comes to our tables. Other chemicals in food come from preservatives used in the foods themselves and in packing them.

We are exposed to chemicals even in our clothes. Chemicals are used in fabric factories to make clothes wrinkle-free or easier to wash or longer-wearing or more lastingly dyed. Our houses, too, are built with factory-made, chemically treated materials, such as insulation in the walls.

Roofers do work that exposes them to carcinogens.
Understanding where the carcinogens may come from can
help workers guard against them.

These industrial chemicals enter our environment with no intention on anyone's part to cause harm. The suspicion that overexposure to some chemicals causes cancer is very recent. Many chemicals have now been tested, and most do not cause cancer.

Doctors now study diseases in relation to how people live and work. This study, called *epidemiology*, is an important part of cancer research. Doctors map geographic locations where certain cancers occur most often. They try to match cancer cases with common experiences such as eating particular foods or working in certain situations. If the epidemiologists find a higher-than-normal rate of cancer among certain workers, they look for causes. Perhaps the cause is in the workers' tools, materials, or methods. It was in this way that doctors discovered that asbestos caused cancer among shipbuilders and construction workers. With such information people can think of ways to protect themselves.

One important project is collecting statistics from places around the world. Where the occurrence of a particular type of cancer is especially high, scientists search for causes in the environment or the lifestyle of the people. They have found causes of cancer in many things besides industrial pollutants. In Africa, for instance, the way farmers stored peanuts accounted for the growth of a cancer-causing substance.

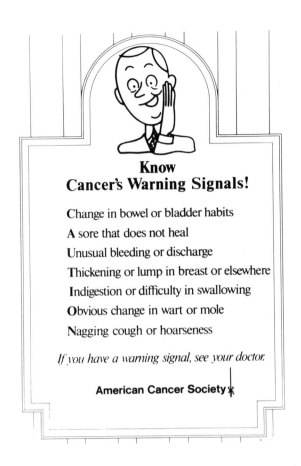

**Know
Cancer's Warning Signals!**

Change in bowel or bladder habits
A sore that does not heal
Unusual bleeding or discharge
Thickening or lump in breast or elsewhere
Indigestion or difficulty in swallowing
Obvious change in wart or mole
Nagging cough or hoarseness

If you have a warning signal, see your doctor.

American Cancer Society

Some people have mixed feelings about these efforts. Manufacturers, for instance, fear that they will be required to spend large sums of money to rebuild factories. Workers fear cancer investigations will end in a factory close down which could cost them their jobs. City or county governments do not move as swiftly as some people want against sources of pollution. Local government officials fear that a factory, rather than cleaning up its environment, will simply move elsewhere.

For reasons like these, state and local governments have problems when they try to pass laws against known *carcinogens*, agents which cause cancer. Some of these efforts must be nationwide to be effective. Yet it would be difficult to restrict the use of every kind of chemical that might cause cancer. People working against these laws point out that not very much is known or proven. They say that people have panicked because of the fear of cancer, not because of the evidence.

A concerned person need not wait for the federal government to pass laws. Even without the majority agreement that getting laws passed requires, we can do a great deal to protect ourselves.

We can probably avoid some cancers by living as healthy a life as we can. "Moderation in all things" is a rule that ancient Greeks formulated several thousand years ago, long before the first test-tube. It is still a good rule. Here are some others closer to our time:

Let's not smoke.

Avoid getting sunburned. Wearing a sun-screening lotion or simply staying out of the sun can save us from skin cancers.

Avoid using chemicals in the house or garden when they are not necessary.

Eat wholesome food. According to some studies, a diet with too much fat and not enough whole grains has contributed to some cancers in the United States.

Laurence Le Shan, a psychologist who worked with many cancer patients, believed that mental attitudes make a difference to one's health, too. He found that gloomy, discouraged people seemed to recover more slowly than others. While not every scientist agrees, some do think that mental outlook influences health.

When someone is sick, a "good attitude" means more than a pleasant smile. It also means having courage. We can become more courageous when we have to. Cancer patients need courage, and their families do, too. They need strength to stay close to an ill person. It takes a special kind of bravery to share another's thoughts and feelings when that sharing is painful.

Sometimes the well people want to run away. They leave the room. They are too busy to visit. Or they are too interested in what they are saying to listen to the other person.

It is natural and normal to feel sad, frightened, or rebellious. It is natural to cry sometimes. It is all right to have these feelings. A serious illness is an ordeal. When someone in our family—or perhaps oneself—is seriously ill, we can look around to see how others bear their burdens so we can try to be as strong.

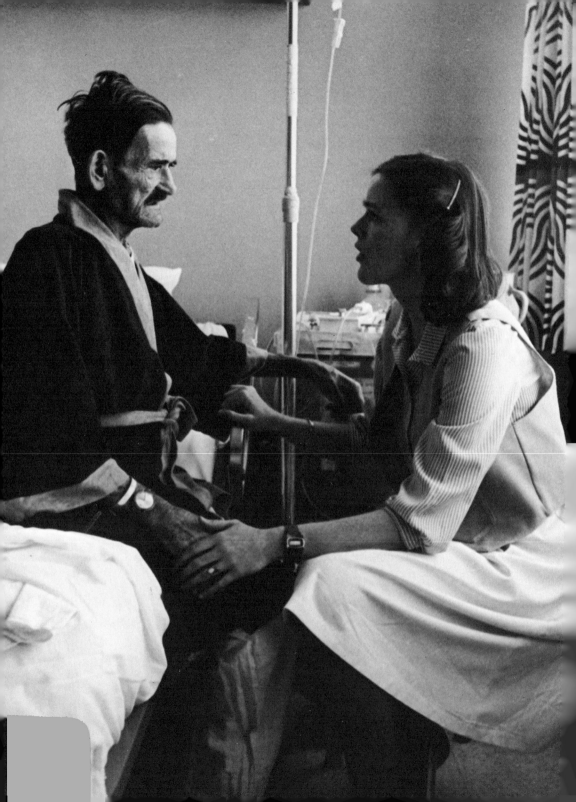

When someday all cancers are curable, the fear will dwindle. But with our own actions and attitudes, we can make cancer less fearsome right now.

Mary Ann's grandmother feels well now. She goes to the doctor for checkups. Otherwise her life is the same as it was, except that she enjoys it more. She and Mary Ann laugh and talk and go places, just as before. Grandmother has decided that there is no reason to worry now, so she will not worry. And since Grandmother feels that way, so does Mary Ann.

Hospital worker talks with a cancer patient.

DISTRIBUTION OF CANCER IN THE U.S.
(TOTAL: 811,000 NEWLY REPORTED PATIENTS IN 1981)

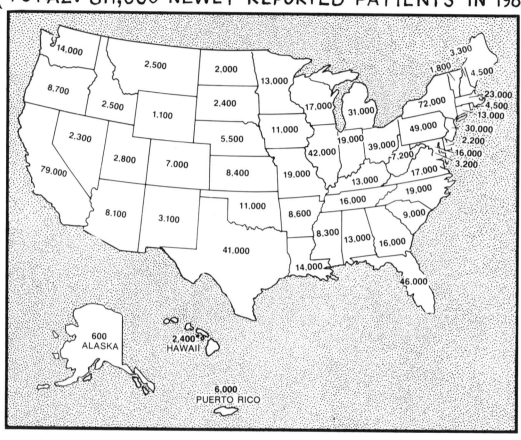

FOR FURTHER INFORMATION

American Cancer Society, Inc.
777 Third Avenue
New York, New York 10017
212-371-2900

Office of Cancer Communications
National Cancer Institute
Bethesda, Maryland 20205
Toll-free telephone number: 800-638-6694

Organizations of patients and families of patients who
wish to help each other:

The Candlelighters Foundation
2025 Eye Street, NW
Washington, DC 20006

Make Today Count
P.O. Box 303
Burlington, Iowa 52601
319-753-6112
319-754-8977

CHUMS (Cancer Hopefuls United for
Mutual Support)
A national coalition of cancer
survivors united for mutual support
3310 Rochambeau Ave.
New York, N.Y. 10467

GLOSSARY

Cancer—a disease resulting from uncontrolled reproduction of cells. Cancers occur in plants and animals as well as humans. There are about 100 different kinds of human cancer.

Carcinogen—a cancer-causing agent.

Cell—the smallest living unit that can exist by itself. Whether plant or animal, a cell contains a nucleus and is covered by a thin membrane. Cells live, grow, take in food, give off wastes, use energy, reproduce, and die.

Chemotherapy—an attack on cancer by use of a drug.

Chromosome—a threadlike structure in a cell's nucleus that is made of DNA and contains genes.

DNA—deoxyribonucleic acid, a chemical substance in chromosomes that controls the life process.

Gene—the combinations of DNA that determine the characteristics of a cell's descendants.

Genetic—concerning genes or heredity.

Immunology—the study of how the body resists disease.

Interferon—a substance produced by human cells in defense against some viruses and chemicals.

Leukemia—a kind of cancer in the blood.

Membrane—a very thin covering that encloses a cell. A membrane also covers the nucleus and some of a cell's other parts.

Metastasize—to spread from one part of the body to another.

Molecule—the smallest possible part of a substance that cannot be further divided without changing its nature.

Nucleus—the control center of a cell. It may not be at the exact physical center.

Operation—an act of surgery.

Proteins—the chemical substances of which cells are mostly made.

Radiation—an attack on cancer by use of rays from substances such as radium.

Radium—an element discovered by Pierre and Marie Curie which is found in minerals and ores that contain uranium.

Surgeon—a physician specially trained to do surgery or manual procedures on the body.

Surgery—the treatment of injury or disease by a manual procedure. It usually means removing or rearranging part of the body.

Tissue—a group of specialized cells that has a particular function in a body, such as muscle tissue. Different kinds of tissues form organs, such as lungs.

INDEX